01

IX

D0946462

PET OWNER'S GUIDE TO THE
GERBIL

Brian Dew

RINGPRESS

**Published by Ringpress Books Limited,
PO Box 8, Lydney, Gloucestershire,
GL15 4YN, United Kingdom.**

First published 2001
©2001 Ringpress Books Limited. All rights reserved

Design: Rob Benson

ISBN 1 86054 183 6

Printed and bound in Hong Kong through Printworks International Ltd.

CONTENTS

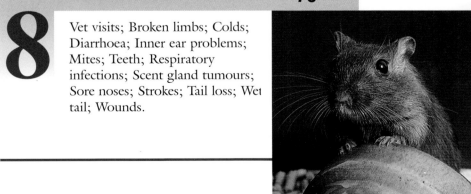

1 Introducing The Gerbil

Gerbils are small animals, about 12 centimetres (5 inches) in length, with long, furry tails that are themselves almost another 12 cms long. They have large, dark eyes, and long, muscular hind legs, which allow them to dig and jump incredibly well.

The gerbil's Latin name, Meriones unguiculatus, means 'clawed warrior'. The gerbil is a member of the rodent family and is similar to other rodents in many ways.

Gerbils have many interesting behaviours and qualities which make them an excellent choice of pet, particularly for children.

INTRODUCING THE GERBIL

There are many species of gerbils, most of which live in hot, dry, and barren areas. The gerbil is well adapted to its desert habitat, having excellent hearing with which to detect predators, and the ability to eat a wide variety of foods, while also requiring very little water.

In the wild, gerbils eat seeds, roots, flowers, and various plants. Some species of gerbils are known to hoard food in their burrows, which can be very useful when food becomes scarce. Gerbils in captivity, however, are not known to hoard their food, probably because they are given food regularly. Gerbils can absorb water through the vegetable matter they digest. Any excess water is then stored in the body in layers of fat, in a similar fashion to the way camels store water in their humps. When water resources are very low, this stored water can be used to keep the gerbil alive.

It is so difficult to survive in this harsh, dry habitat that the gerbil has very few natural enemies in the wild.

Consequently, it is a strong and stable species in places such as Asia, Northern Africa, and the Middle East.

HISTORY

Little is known about the evolutionary history of the gerbil. Gerbils were first discovered in China, and later to the east of Mongolia. In 1935, the first gerbils were captured and taken from their natural habitat, but it was not until 20 years later that they reached western countries like Britain and America.

In 1954, scientist Dr Victor Schwentker took some gerbils to the United States to be used for research. It was while the gerbils were being kept in cages in the laboratory that staff realised what wonderful pets gerbils made. Since then, they have been commonly kept as pets.

DIFFERENT VARIETIES

There are many different varieties of gerbils. The most common, in the wild, is the Mongolian. The Mongolian Gerbil is the one most commonly kept as a pet, but there are about 90 other species from which to choose. Recently, jirds (a type of gerbil) have become more popular, in particular Shaw's Jirds.

Shaw's Jirds are similar in size to a rat or squirrel, and look like a giant gerbil. Much like Mongolian Gerbils, Shaw's Jirds make wonderful pets. They are very

The Mongolian Gerbil is the type that is most commonly kept as a pet.

intelligent, and, being larger than Mongolian Gerbils, easier to pet and cuddle.

The one major difference between Shaw's Jirds and other gerbils is that the former require small amounts of meat in their diet (mealworms will suffice). Shaws's Jirds also require a larger aquarium, because of their bigger size.

BEHAVIOUR

Unlike the hamster, and many other desert animals, gerbils are not nocturnal – a feature which makes them an ideal choice for a pet. Due to the daytime heat of the desert, wild gerbils will stay in the burrows they dig throughout the day, sometimes sleeping and sometimes being active.

Gerbils dig very long and complex sets of tunnels, which include nest areas, and places to store food.

The tunnels have many entrances, allowing for an easy escape in case of danger, and are usually dug beneath plants, so that the plant roots support the ceilings of the tunnels.

Burrows vary in size and complexity, ranging from a single tunnel on its own, to warrens of tunnels with numerous 'rooms'.

Each burrow will only house members of the same family. Any gerbil who is not a member of the occupying family is likely to be attacked if it enters the tunnel. This is because gerbils are very territorial, defending their own territories vigorously.

Even when looking for food,

gerbils will generally stay near their burrows. This is to avoid dangerous predators that may be lurking. Desert conditions mean that there is little in the way of natural cover, so the safest alternative is to remain within easy striking distance of the tunnel entrances.

Gerbils are very exciting and lively animals, always interested in their surroundings. They take a keen interest in what is going on around them and will usually investigate new sounds or objects rather than running and hiding.

Gerbils are not at all timid and are extremely curious. A gerbil will normally investigate something rather than attack it, which is why they rarely bite while being held.

COMMUNICATION

Gerbils communicate in a similar fashion to rabbits. If a gerbil is in a dangerous situation, it will often thump its hind legs. It does this by standing up straight and very quickly tapping its hind feet on the ground.

This is used to warn other gerbils of trouble, and they will commonly thump back in response, or quickly run away from the danger. In this way, news spreads throughout the whole group very quickly.

Active and inquisitive, the gerbil takes an interest in everything that is going on.

Gerbils have a unique system of communication to warn each other of imminent danger.

Gerbils may also thump as a mating ritual, but the thumping is usually a lot quicker and not as loud. This warning system, which gerbils use in the wild, is very effective because many of the gerbil's predators are birds, which can attack quickly. By passing the information through the entire group, gerbils can be warned before they are aware of danger, allowing them to retreat into their tunnels.

FURTHER INFORMATION

If you think that gerbils may be the pet for you, but want more information before you make the decision, there are several avenues you can follow.

Vets, gerbil breeders, and pet shops will usually be happy to answer any questions you may have. An alternative, valuable resource is the Internet, which hosts many gerbil-oriented web sites.

A gerbil will stand upright and thump his hind legs as a warning.

THE NATIONAL GERBIL SOCIETY

A good site at which to start your Internet search belongs to the National Gerbil Society, and can be found at: <http://www.rodent.demon.co.uk/index.htm>.

The National Gerbil Society was founded in 1970 and is one of the leading authorities on gerbils. It was founded in Great Britain, although membership is available to people of all nationalities.

The purpose of the society is to promote the keeping of gerbils and jirds as pets, and the importance of proper care.

The National Gerbil Society holds judging shows – a sort of gerbil equivalent to Crufts – from which the winning gerbils receive trophies and rosettes. Rules, breed standards, and membership details can be found on its web site.

The web site also contains general information all about gerbils, details about different breeds, recent research, evaluations of materials, and tips on how to ensure your gerbils are well looked after.

Other web sites, which are relevant to anyone interested in gerbils, are also mentioned.

You can find out more about gerbils by searching the Internet.

2 *Setting Up Home*

Before choosing a gerbil and bringing it home, you should have already bought and prepared a cage for the gerbil's arrival. Having a cage prepared is very important. It can be very difficult to set up the cage and make sure the gerbil does not escape from its temporary carrier!

The cage should be in a room where the temperature does not vary too much, and should not be placed in direct sunlight, or be in the path of draughts or breezes. It should also be out of the reach of dogs, cats, and other animals that may bother the gerbil. If very young children are present, it is a good idea to make sure the cage is out of their reach.

CAGES
There are many different types and sizes of cage available. They range from small, plastic, box types to large, elaborate and expensive ones, sometimes connected with a series of tunnels, and designed to recreate the gerbil's natural environment. Whichever cage is chosen, one basic consideration should be borne in mind: the more gerbils the cage is expected to house, the bigger the cage should be. Each individual gerbil should have a bare-minimum space of 35 sq cm (13 sq inches). It is also worth remembering that some cages are better suited to younger gerbils, while others may be more suitable for older gerbils which are less mobile. For example, younger gerbils require more space in which to run around, and can get a lot of enjoyment from running through tunnels or climbing ladders. Older gerbils may become distressed if too much agility is required to move around inside the cage. They may be better suited to a plain aquarium-style cage.

PLASTIC CAGES
The simplest cage is the plastic

Small plastic cages should be used as carry cases only.

cage with a vented plastic top. These cages are commonly used to keep reptiles, and sometimes hamsters and mice. They are very inexpensive and make excellent travelling boxes, but are not suitable to use as a gerbil's main residence. The standard size of this type of cage is far too small for a pair or group of gerbils, and the plastic is easily gnawed by a gerbil's constantly growing teeth.

METAL WIRE CAGES

Another type of cage which is very common is the metal wire cage. These can be bought in many sizes and with many different levels. They usually have a plastic base. This cage has many good features

but, if chosen without care, it can be dangerous to gerbils. It is important to choose a cage which has plain metal bars, which are not painted. This is because the gerbils may eat the paint, which can make them very ill.

The advantages of the wire cage include its excellent ventilation (air flows freely through the bars and circulates throughout the cage) and its easiness to clean. Most of these types of cages have a removable tray in the bottom, which can just be pulled out, with all the soiled wood shavings in it, emptied, washed, new shavings added, and replaced. The wire cage also offers gerbils the chance

A metal wire cage provides excellent air circulation.

to gnaw and shorten their teeth. However, care should be taken that this does not lead to the gerbil developing a sore nose as a result of pushing it through the bars.

One of the disadvantages of choosing a wire cage is the mess that a gerbil can make when housed in it. Gerbils will commonly push shavings and nesting material out through the bars. This may be nothing more than a minor irritation, but if toddlers come into the room and eat the discarded bedding, it can become a very serious problem.

Wire cages can actually be dangerous for gerbils, when insufficient care is given to their location. If the cage is left in a draught, the cold air will move freely around the cage, as the lack of solid sides means there is little insulation. If the temperature gets cold enough, the gerbil may freeze to death.

AQUARIUMS

One of the best types of cage is the glass or plastic aquarium. For a pair of gerbils a 10- to 20-US gallon (38- to 76-litre) aquarium is ideal. The glass walls allow the cage to be filled almost to the top

The gerbil's natural habitat can be recreated with a glass or plastic aquarium.

with wood shavings, sand or sawdust (see Wood Shavings, page 17). This allows the gerbils to tunnel and to build their own nests, so recreating their natural habitat as far as is possible. Gerbils may dig next to the side of the aquarium, making it easy to see the insides of a gerbil tunnel and providing a great source of educational fun for children.

Unlike wire cages, aquariums hold nesting material and wood shavings inside them very well, and with a ventilated top they can still provide plenty of air for the gerbils. Aquariums are also the perfect cage for pregnant gerbils and new-borns.

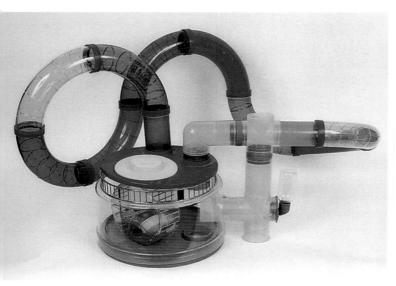

Modular cages are colourful and can provide hours of entertainment.

MULTI-COMPONENT CAGES

A more expensive and complicated cage is the cage made up of several separate but interconnecting parts, which are connected with plastic tunnels. Although this cage is expensive, very difficult to clean, and takes up a large amount of space, it is the most fun for the gerbils. This cage provides hours of fun and exploration for gerbils, which can constantly crawl through a series of tunnels to different rooms. There are many interesting attachments to these cages, including play-rooms and mazes. Some of the cages in this range come with snap-on wheels, water bottles, and food dispensers.

Some problems have been reported with this type of cage. Complaints have been made that tunnels can be chewed through too easily, resulting in an escaped gerbil or frequent bills for the owner. However, anti-gnaw rings can be bought from most pet shops to overcome this problem. The rings are made of metal and fit on the ends of the tunnel.

Another problem is that the design of the cages is not particularly suitable for very young or very old gerbils – the tunnels can prove too difficult for them to traverse. However, ladders (originally aimed at making the cages suitable for dwarf hamsters), can solve this. The ladders have hooks on the end that slip over the edge of the tunnel and then descend through the tunnel. This gives young and elderly gerbils the ability to travel through the tunnel safely and easily.

THE RIGHT CAGE

Whichever cage you decide to buy, it should be the biggest you can afford. It should also be checked to make sure it is escape-proof and safe. Gerbils are notorious for escaping. Make sure there are no loose wires or other sharp objects in the cage. Apart from the fact that gerbils can use these to create or enlarge a hole through which they can escape, these sharp objects can seriously injure a gerbil.

FLOOR COVERINGS

The floor of the gerbils' cage should have a layer of wood shavings, sawdust, or other floor covering. This layer is used to absorb the gerbil's waste products.

WOOD SHAVINGS

Wood shavings do not absorb waste as well as sawdust, but sawdust is known to irritate gerbils. The shavings purchased should be those intended for use with small animals because shavings purchased through a sawmill company may contain a great deal of dust, which can be harmful to gerbils. Aspen shavings are highly recommended. This is due to the fact that there are reports that pine and cedar shavings have not only caused respiratory infection, but also the death of some baby gerbils.

When wood shavings are placed inside the cage, they should cover the whole of the cage floor in a thin layer. Where the gerbil is known to defecate, and where the water bottle is placed, extra shavings should be added to absorb waste products and any spillage. If you want to let your gerbils burrow, a larger amount of wood shavings needs to be added. In this case, it is important to use a cage with high, solid sides, so that it is not kicked out.

Make sure the wood shavings you buy are suitable for small animals.

ALTERNATIVE FLOOR COVERINGS

If desired, you can make your own floor covering, from ground-up corncobs. This works very well, and is safe for the gerbils. Sand is also a possibility, but can sometimes irritate a gerbil's eyes and nose. This may sound surprising, since the gerbil's natural habitat is one of sand, but it is the fact that gerbils in cages are not in their natural environment that makes sand unsuitable. Sand works very well in allowing gerbils to tunnel, but does not work at all well when it comes to absorbing gerbils' waste. In the wild, gerbils would leave the tunnel system or use a particular area to defecate. In captivity, they do not have this option.

Items from the garden or outdoors should never be used inside in a gerbil's cage, e.g. using soil as a substitute for wood shavings. This is because gerbils are susceptible to infections caused by mites and many outdoor items contain lots of mites.

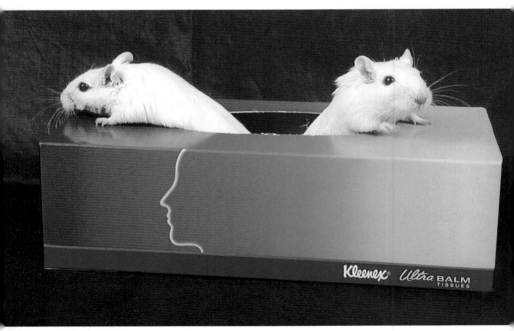

Cardboard boxes can be used for play and then chewed up to make a nest.

NESTING MATERIAL

Gerbils should have some material in their cage that they can chew up to make a nest for them to sleep in.

ITEMS FROM THE HOME

Tissues work well as a nesting material, because they are very soft and can be chewed up in seconds. Gerbils also enjoy cardboard toilet-paper rolls, and paper-towel rolls. A gerbil will chew up the tissues or cardboard rolls, and sleep in a nest made out of the chewed-up materials.

Newspaper is not safe for gerbils and should not be added to their cage, because the ink on newspaper contains many dyes that can be harmful to them.

PAPER WOOL

Commercially-produced nesting materials can be purchased in packets. Examples include paper wool, which is similar to cotton-wool (cotton). However, unlike cotton wool, paper wool consists of synthetic fibres rather than natural fibres. Paper wool is a safe nesting material for most small animals, and offers good value for money, due to the fact that it expands considerably when removed from the packet and

Paper bedding provides extra warmth.

placed in the gerbils' nest.

If you prefer this type of bedding, always buy it from a pet shop. Using ordinary cotton wool as a substitute is dangerous – gerbils are known to choke on it. Paper wool works well and when some is placed in the gerbils' cage they will make it into a nest fairly quickly. Paper wool will also keep the gerbils warmer than other substances can. However, the first few times this particular nesting material is used, observe your gerbils carefully. Some gerbils have choked on this material.

OTHER MATERIALS

Regular wool, and all cloths or plastics, may harm gerbils. Gerbils can get caught in these substances and suffocate, or get their limbs tangled in these materials, resulting in serious injuries or even

Gerbils love toys that they can climb on or run through.

materials. By far the safer and cheaper option is to use tissues and cardboard rolls.

CAGE FURNISHINGS

Gerbils love to run around and play in their cages, and a few simple toys can make a gerbil's cage complete. However, do not overfill the cage with toys, as the gerbils should always have room to run around, and to make a nest. Many types of toys, wheels, and houses are available for sale at most pet shops, but it is important to know which type to purchase. Anything constructed of plastic, such as houses, will be chewed up by the gerbil is a very short amount of time. Play toys should be made of a more durable material, such as wood.

death. There are many options for nesting materials, but nearly all have been known to cause problems for gerbils. It is therefore important to use good judgement in selecting safe products for your gerbils' nesting

Play toys, like these, must be made of durable material.

HOUSES AND TOYS

A simple glass jar or clay pot can make a suitable home for gerbils and they are very inexpensive. A wooden cube with holes through each side makes a wonderful toy, and, if food dishes and other important objects in the cage are placed on top of the wood block, they are less likely to get knocked over, or covered up with bedding.

Cardboard boxes are suitable and inexpensive toys. When the gerbils have finished playing with them and chewing them, they will use the cardboard in their nest. Be creative but cautious in the toys you give to your gerbils.

EXERCISE WHEELS

Exercise wheels come as standard with many cages, and make an excellent toy for gerbils, helping to keep them healthy. However, there are many different types of wheels and it is important to choose the right one. They should be made out of metal, and not painted. If the gerbils chew the wheel and swallow the paint, they can become very ill. A gerbil's long tail getting caught in the wheel is a hazard, but not a very common one, and can be avoided by buying a solid wheel or weaving cardboard through the wheel rungs.

If your gerbils get a lot of use out of the wheel, it is best to purchase either a cage with a wheel already incorporated, or a wheel which can be firmly attached to the side of the cage. Free-standing wheels can be overturned very easily.

Some household objects can be adapted as toys for your gerbil.

3 *Choosing Your Gerbil*

Gerbils are relatively inexpensive to buy, very friendly and sociable, and require little in the way of care. However, although gerbils are very clean and self-sufficient animals, they still require some degree of care and responsibility.

Before you buy one or choose to give one as a gift to a child, make sure that the gerbil can be properly cared for.

Gerbils provide excellent value for money. Their almost constant activity means they provide hours of entertainment and fun. They are also very affectionate and lovable pets that give their owners plenty of enjoyment.

Gerbils produce very little smell, especially if their cage is cleaned often, and the standard-sized gerbil cage takes up very little space, making gerbils an ideal pet for the classroom or for someone who lives in a small flat or house.

WHERE TO GET A GERBIL

There are many places where someone can purchase a gerbil, pet shops included. However, by far the best place to find one is through a well-respected gerbil breeder.

If you take on a gerbil, you must cater for all its needs.

A responsible breeder will provide detailed information about the gerbils that are for sale.

BREEDERS

A good breeder will be able to supply you with a gerbil for which exact information is known about its date of birth and its parentage. The breeder should be able to answer any questions you may have pertaining to breeding and care.

Breeders can be found on the Internet, but if you are unable to find one local to you, try asking at your local pet shop. Many pet shops buy their gerbils from a breeder, and should be able to put you in contact with a breeder living locally.

PET SHOPS

Most pet shops will sell gerbils, and some will have a variety of colours in stock, but pet shops will not generally carry as many varieties of gerbils as a gerbil breeder. If you buy your first gerbil from a pet store, always make sure that the gerbil has been kept in clean conditions and is well fed before you purchase it. It is also important to check that the pet shop routinely separates its males and females, so that you do not end up taking home a pregnant female, or a gerbil cruelly separated from his mate. When purchasing a gerbil from a pet store, check the other gerbils in the cage for signs of injury or sickness, and make sure all the gerbils appear to be healthy and active.

As a source of gerbils, a high-quality pet shop is the best alternative to a breeder. A good shop should have at least one trained member of staff who is knowledgeable about all the animals they sell and can guide you through the purchase, helping you to make an informed decision.

OTHER SOURCES

Although breeders and pet shops are the recommended sources for gerbils, there are other alternatives available. Animal shelters nearly always have a high number of small animals in their care, gerbils among them. Although the history of gerbils from this source may be uncertain, most will still live to average age, and the new owner can take a great deal of satisfaction from knowing they have given the gerbils a second chance.

If you take a look at any notice boards in local shops, you will frequently find 'homes wanted' advertisements for gerbils and other small animals. These are usually the result of an unexpected pregnancy. Gerbils acquired in this manner may make excellent pets if they have been well cared for. Ask to view the parents in their cages and normal surroundings. If the cages are clean and roomy, and the gerbils seem to be active and happy, there is no reason why you cannot purchase gerbils in this manner.

An unplanned pregnancy can result in gerbils being advertised for sale locally.

Male gerbil.

Female gerbil.

MALE OR FEMALE?

Male gerbils are generally less aggressive than female gerbils, but females can be just as calm as males, especially with regular handling. Unless you want to breed gerbils, it is a good idea to get two gerbils of the same sex. In this case, it is best if they come from the same litter.

Generally, there is little difference between keeping male or female gerbils. It is entirely a matter of personal choice. However, whichever sex you decide on, make sure that the sex of each gerbil you buy is absolutely certain, otherwise you may end up with far more gerbils than you bargained for!

SEXING

As with many small animals, it is very easy to sex gerbils incorrectly.

Even so-called experts can get it wrong occasionally. For this reason, it is always a good idea to perform a double-check and sex your gerbils yourself when you bring them home. It is particularly important to do this if you have purchased your gerbils from a pet shop as opposed to a breeder.

To sex gerbils, hold them firmly by the base of their tail, supporting their back with your other hand, and turn them so that their underside is presented to you. Check to see whether the underside looks more like the male or female genitalia seen in the photographs here. Females are recognisable by the short distance between their anus and vaginal vent, whereas the male has such a short gap between his anus and the penile vent that the two are often indistinguishable. The male can also be identified by having a puffed-up appearance about his genitalia, due to the fact that this is where the testes are stored internally.

HOW MANY?

Gerbils are very sociable animals and should always be kept in pairs or groups. Gerbils who are kept alone will become very unhappy, symptoms of which include quiet and listless behaviour.

Lonely gerbils also feel very unsafe, and are consequently more inclined to bite. This is due to fear and uncertainty. As there is no other gerbil present, there is no communication, and no communication means the gerbil has no way of knowing that the approaching human does not pose a threat. A gerbil in this situation may decide to get in its attack before the human can!

The only restriction on the number of gerbils (upwards of two) which you can keep is how much money you have to spend on cages or cage extensions. Gerbils can live in very large groups but need to have as much space as possible. As a guide, a pair of adult gerbils can live in a 38-litre (10-US-gallon) aquarium.

PAIR-BONDS

Gerbils can be kept in very large groups, although this is usually a more peaceful state of affairs if all the gerbils are from the same litter. If you want to keep a large group

If you do not plan to breed your gerbils, the best solution is to keep a same-sex pair.

of gerbils, it is wise to ensure that the gerbils are kept in multiples of two, as opposed to uneven numbers. It is also important to keep the gerbils sexually segregated. Not only does this eliminate the risk of unwanted pregnancies, but it also avoids conflict. Mixed-sex, odd-numbered groups will fight. For example, if two females and a male are kept together, there is a high risk that the two females will fight for the male. They may end up killing each other, and even if everything seems fine initially, they will fight eventually.

Another reason for keeping gerbils in multiples of two is that the pair-bond is a natural state for the gerbil. This bond goes far beyond that of simple playmates. The gerbils will sleep cuddled up together and will also groom each other – a very intimate act.

If you are not planning on breeding gerbils, a same-sex pair-bond is the best solution. Preferably, these two gerbils should be from the same litter, so that they are already familiar with each other's scent.

HOME-COMING
Once you have prepared the cage for your gerbils' arrival and have added fresh food and water (see Chapters Two and Four), it is time to introduce your new friends. When the gerbils are brought home they should be taken gently out of the travelling box, and placed in the cage. It will take some time for them to adapt to their new environment, and to you, so they should be left in peace for a day or two, allowing them to settle in and make a nest. The gerbils will run around exploring their new home for some time, pushing bedding around and moving it into the area they want.

After two or three days, once the gerbils have had time to settle in, it is advisable to introduce yourself to the gerbils and accustom them to being handled by you (see Chapter Four). If you do not, you may end up with unfriendly gerbils that will bite you as often as they greet you.

HANDLING GERBILS
Although gerbils should be allowed a few days to settle into their new surroundings, regular handling should begin shortly after purchase. Gerbils which are used to handling will hardly ever bite and are very affectionate. Gerbils which are not handled

Hand-feeding is the best way of establishing trust between gerbil and owner.

frequently will be fearful of the experience, and respond the only way they know how – with a nip.

It may help to allow the gerbils to become familiar with your scent before you hold them. Feeding them treats by hand is a very effective way of achieving this. Put an open hand with a treat placed on the palm inside the gerbil's cage, and let the hand rest there until the gerbil walks over to investigate. Eventually it will take the treat, and before long will associate the scent of its owner with something it likes, i.e. a treat. When the gerbil becomes accustomed to your scent, you will

be able to hold it more easily, and should not get bitten.

PICKING UP YOUR GERBIL

After the gerbil has had time to get used to its new surroundings and owner, it may be picked up and held frequently without difficulty. To pick up a gerbil for the first time, remove the top of the cage. Using both hands, scoop up the gerbil in your palms (do not be surprised if it runs away at first). Once the gerbil is in your hands slowly lift it out of the cage. Make sure you do this gently and do not lift the gerbil too far from the ground. If it becomes frightened, the gerbil may jump, injuring or even killing itself.

Ideally, the gerbil should be picked up while you are in a sitting position, so that if it jumps, falls or is dropped, it will land on the relatively soft cushion of your lap. If a gerbil tries to jump, it may be better to let it do so, as long as it is on to a soft surface. This is because, in trying to prevent the gerbil from jumping, you may inadvertently hurt it by squeezing too hard. A gerbil is surprisingly vulnerable to even a gentle squeeze.

Once the gerbil has become accustomed to being picked up

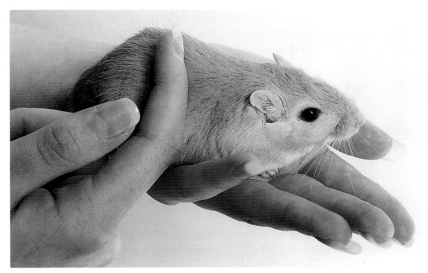

Take your time, and be very gentle when handling a gerbil.

and handled, you may like to let it run from one hand to the other. This gives the gerbil more freedom and more opportunity to investigate you and the outside world. If doing this, however, make sure that you are fully alert and that you still have control over the gerbil. You need to be ready to catch your gerbil should it try to escape.

So long as you take care to be gentle, you may hold the gerbil in cupped hands and stroke its fur. If done properly, without frightening it, most gerbils really like this experience. If yours does, you should find that it runs to you when you place your hand in the cage. This is a sign of affection and trust.

INTRODUCING GERBILS

If only one gerbil is purchased at first, you may want to add a mate for this gerbil, so that it does not become lonely later on. Although it is better to buy gerbils in pairs, preferably from the same litter, if you want to introduce a strange gerbil, try to make sure it is of similar size and age to the existing gerbil. This ensures that one of the gerbils will not feel immediately intimidated and respond aggressively. It is more than likely that the gerbils will fight on first introduction, as each tries to establish dominance, but it may be best to let them carry on (unless one of them is in danger) until the matter is resolved.

If you are introducing another gerbil in this fashion, try to do so when your existing gerbil is still young. Young gerbils tend to be less aggressive and less prone towards fighting, because they have not yet fully developed a scent to mark their territory. Introducing two gerbils to each other at a young age is usually a fairly peaceful process.

GENERATION GAPS

If you want to introduce an older gerbil to a younger gerbil, more care needs to be taken.

Clean the cage and the toys, and rearrange everything in the cage. This process substantially reduces the older gerbil's scent, making the cage more neutral and less intimidating to the new gerbil. It also makes the older gerbil less sure of its surroundings so that it does not react quite so aggressively to the new arrival. Putting the two gerbils together

Introduce gerbils to each other when they are young, as they will be less aggressive.

in this 'new' cage should then hopefully be quite a peaceful event.

Nevertheless, even with this technique, there is a possibility that they will fight, and the gerbils should be closely watched for a short time after being introduced. A sign to look out for when you introduce gerbils is whether they stand on their back legs and appear to be boxing each other. This means they are going to fight.

Other signs of aggression are when one gerbil chases the other aggressively around the cage, or if one gerbil lets out a loud squeaking sound. When gerbils roll around in a ball, this means they are fighting and attempting to kill each other. They must be separated at once or one will die.

The person who separates the fighting gerbils will undoubtedly get bitten, but it must be done. It is a good idea to keep a pair of gardening gloves next to the cage for this reason.

ADULT INTRODUCTIONS

Introducing two adult gerbils is best not attempted. It has a high failure rate. However, if an owner really wants two adult gerbils to share a cage, one method is to use a wire-mesh cage divider that vertically separates the cage in two.

A gerbil is placed on either side of this cage, and will eventually get to know the other gerbil's scent. If necessary, the side each gerbil is on can be switched every day.

After a while you should be able to safely remove the divider. You should always be cautious and observe the gerbils to make sure they are getting along, however, before leaving them unsupervised.

Introductions should not be rushed. If the first introduction is successful, repeat it on a couple of occasions. The gerbils need to spend some time being introduced to each other before they will stay together, and if they are separated when they engage in little fights, it may take longer for them to become comfortable living together.

When gerbils are put in their new home for the first time, it is important to watch them carefully to make sure they are not injuring each other and cannot escape.

4 *Caring For Your Gerbils*

As a caring, responsible gerbil owner, there are several routines to follow. You must:
- Change food and water daily
- Clean the cage, at least weekly
- Perform regular 'check-ups' on all your gerbils, just to make sure that everything is as it should be (see Health Checks, page 39).

FEEDING
Gerbils should be fed every day, and if necessary twice a day, depending on how many gerbils are in the cage. As a general rule, the more gerbils, the more food will be consumed. A handful of food should suffice for each feed and should either be spread across the floor of the cage, or placed in a food bowl. If your gerbils prefer to eat their food off the floor, remember to remove food which has not been consumed shortly afterwards, so as to avoid infection from the bedding.

For most gerbils, feeding once a day will be adequate. If the food disappears immediately, it is usually better to add more food per feed than to switch to twice-daily feeding. Twice-daily feeding is normally practised only when large groups of gerbils are kept in the same cage. The principle behind feeding more often is that it offers a second chance to gerbils which may have missed out on the first feed. To assess whether or not your gerbils require twice-daily feeding, check to see whether all the gerbils can gain access to the food before it disappears. If they cannot, and increasing the size of the feed does not help, you should switch to twice-daily feeding.

DRIED FOOD
Pre-mixed gerbil foods offer the main and most important part of a gerbil's diet. These mixtures contain different varieties of seeds, corn kernels and pellets, and

provide many of the essential nutrients necessary for the health of your gerbils. Most pet shops sell these ready-mixed foods either in pre-packaged bags (usually labelled with the types of animal for which the feed is suitable), or loose in tubs. Be careful if purchasing your feed from tubs. These open food bins, where the customer scoops out the food and pays by weight, may contain mites which are hazardous to gerbils. If purchasing your food in this manner, be sure to thoroughly freeze and then defrost the food before giving it to the gerbils, as this destroys the mites.

OBESITY

The correct weight for an adult gerbil is between 60-130 grams (2-4.5 ounces). Males tend to be heavier than females. Obesity is not a common problem in gerbils, as they rarely tend to overeat. Nevertheless, it is not unknown, and it is a serious condition. As in humans, obesity has significant health implications for gerbils. Extra strain is placed on the heart and a gerbil's life expectancy is reduced.

If a gerbil weighs more than 130g (4.5oz), it is considered obese. It is possible for a gerbil to be obese without appearing noticeably bigger. If your gerbil looks and feels less muscular and firm, this may be an indication of obesity. Typically gerbils will replace muscle-tone with fat, before increasing overall size.

If your gerbils become obese, overfeeding may be the root cause of the problem. However, if reducing the amount of food does not produce the desired response, the combinations of foods in the diet may be responsible. Gerbils should not be given too many fatty seeds, and more healthy foods, such as lettuce and carrots, should be substituted instead.

FRESH FOODS

Vegetables are a good source of nutrients for gerbils, as well as a source of water. Being desert animals, gerbils require very little water and if enough vegetables are provided, gerbils are capable of absorbing all their water needs from vegetables. It is important not to overfeed gerbils with vegetable matter though, as a diet with too many vegetables can cause diarrhoea.

Gerbils will eat many types of vegetables, but it is important to make sure the food is well washed. This ensures that the food is free

Apples should be sliced.

A small amount of cheese adds protein to the diet.

Bananas are a special treat.

Make sure all vegetables are washed.

Pre-mixed complete gerbil foods contain a mix of seeds, corn kernels and pellets.

of pesticides. Like most people, gerbils have different tastes, and will prefer certain foods to others.

Alternative foods which you can give your gerbil are carrots, sliced apples, cucumber and even bananas. These should be put in a separate food bowl. If your gerbil has not eaten these supplements within a few hours of your putting them in the cage, they should be removed. Any fruit or vegetables left in the cage will grow mould, or rot, and possibly cause harm to the gerbils. All food should be prevented as far as possible from having prolonged contact with the bedding. If it does, it may contaminate the food and make the gerbils seriously unwell.

ADDITIONAL FOODS

Gerbils like a wide variety of foods, and it is a good idea to regularly introduce new foods, but make sure they will not harm the gerbil in any way. Some gerbils, especially pregnant or nursing mothers sometimes require some protein in their diets, and they can be given mealworms, which can be purchased at most pet shops.

WATER

Although gerbils are evolved to survive in desert conditions, they still require a constant supply of fresh water. Water bowls should never be used as they are predisposed to spill. Once water has been spilt and covered over with shavings, the cage will smell and a serious health risk is posed to the gerbils. A water bottle is the most suitable way of

providing your gerbils with a fresh supply of water.

Depending on what type of cage is used, there are different types of water bottles. However, all water bottles should be attached to the cage at a level which the gerbil can easily reach. It should not be placed so low that the tip is pressed against the shavings, causing the water to spill out.

Aquariums should use water bottles which are made to hang

A gravity-fed water bottle ensures a constant supply of fresh water.

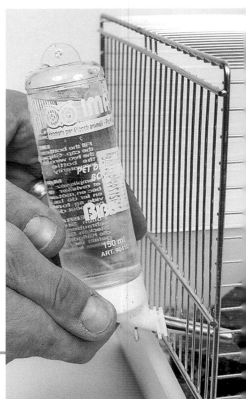

from the wall of the cage or its roof. These are more accessible to gerbils and should therefore be made from glass to avoid being chewed. Metal wire cages can have a water bottle placed on the outside. A metal wire holds the bottle to the cage, and only the drinking spout goes through the bars and into the cage.

Multi-component cages usually come with their own water bottle. Most of the time this can be attached directly to the side of the cage by a special fitting which slots into one of the holes meant for a tunnel. With these type of cages, it is very important to block the hole when refilling the water bottle. The hole offers a very easy escape route for an inquisitive gerbil.

CHECKING THE BOTTLE

Water bottles should be checked daily. Ideally, fresh water should be provided daily also. Once a week, when the cage is cleaned, the water bottle should be washed. Before replacing the water bottle in the cage, always check that it is functioning correctly. Check that it does not leak and that the gerbil is able to suck water through the spout without difficulty. A finger rolled across the tip of the water

A gerbil's cage should be cleaned thoroughly once a week.

bottle will test this. If water comes through and wets the finger then it is functional.

CLEANING THE CAGE

Gerbils should have their cages cleaned at least once a week. If you own a large group of gerbils, you should aim to clean the cage about twice a week. While the cage is being cleaned the gerbils should be kept in an escape-proof box, or travelling box.

All the old wood shavings, nesting material and food should be discarded. After all the old bedding has been disposed of, the cage should be meticulously washed with warm soapy water. Be sure to rinse the cage thoroughly after washing so that the soap does not irritate the

After washing the cage, clean the toys, add fresh bedding material, and fill up the food bowl.

gerbils. Any toys in the gerbils' cage must also be cleaned, with the same soapy solution. This prevents the spread of mites in the cage, a common problem with small animals.

After the cage and toys have been washed, they should be thoroughly dried. The point of washing the bottom of the cage, and toys, is to kill any bacteria which may live under the soiled bedding. The cage does not need to be washed every time the bedding is replaced, but it is a good habit to maintain. When dry, fresh wood shavings and nesting material should be added to the cage, all the cage furnishings should be returned, and fresh food and water should be added.

GROOMING

Gerbils are naturally clean animals and do not need to be groomed by their owners. Much like cats, gerbils groom themselves by licking their paws and rubbing them over their coats. When gerbils are in pairs, they will usually groom each other, and spend far less time grooming themselves.

Gerbils love taking dust baths. A bowl full of chinchilla dust or sand works very well for this purpose. If you observe your gerbils, you should see them rolling around in the dust to remove some of the greasiness from their coats. If, despite the provision of good food and dust-bathing facilities, your gerbil's coat still looks dull, try moving the cage. One of the most powerful factors influencing the quality of a gerbil's coat is air quality. A room with low humidity will restore some of the shine.

HEALTH CHECKS

Every now and then a simple check should be carried out to ensure your gerbils are in good health. The simplest way to perform this quick examination is to inspect the gerbils' droppings, as a great deal of information about the gerbil's general state of health can be gathered from these. The droppings of a healthy gerbil are usually quite dry. Droppings which appear moist may be a sign of diarrhoea, which can be treated with a change of diet, and particularly by giving more dry foods.

Gerbils should also have their teeth checked regularly, to make sure they are not overgrown or broken. Problem teeth may prevent the gerbil from eating and cause it to die from starvation. To check the teeth, the gerbil should be held in a vertical position with its nose pointing up, and the skin on its mouth parted to reveal the teeth.

It is also important to monitor the weight of your gerbil regularly.

Overweight gerbils may be symptomatic of too many sunflower seeds (a very fatty food), whereas skinny gerbils are usually suffering from dehydration, rather than lack of food. This is due to the fact that gerbils store water in layers of fat on their body. If you have an underweight gerbil, check that the water bottle is full of fresh water and functioning correctly.

If you are at all concerned, or notice anything unusual – however innocuous it may seem – consult your vet. He or she will be happy to investigate your concerns.

Check your gerbil's teeth regularly.

RUNNING FREE

You may wish to allow your gerbil to run free every once in a while. This is a good way for the gerbil to get some exercise, and to have a break from the confines of its cage, which prevent it from running about too much.

If you intend to let your gerbil run free, be aware that nothing prevents the gerbils from urinating or defecating on the floor.

The gerbil should only remain loose for a very short period, and should be supervised the whole time. Gerbils can easily chew through electric wires, or escape.

For this reason, it may help to 'fence' off a run area with cushions. Ensure any other pets, such as cats and dogs, are safely confined to a separate room.

It is not a good idea to let gerbils run free outside, for many reasons. Gerbils can pick up mites from the outside, bring them into their cage and infect everything. The gerbils may also consume plants sprayed with pesticide, or poisonous plants. If your gerbil escapes outside, the chances of your being able to catch it are remote, so it is best not to take any chances.

Your gerbil will appreciate a chance to explore what lies beyond his cage.

If you supply plenty of food and water, you can leave your gerbils overnight.

GOING ON HOLIDAY

If you go away on holiday, and are unable to take the gerbils along, it is very important to make sure your pets are properly cared for.

If you are planning on being absent for a short time, such as a weekend or overnight, then the gerbils can be supplied with extra food and water, and should be fine while left alone.

However, even for short trips, it is always important to make sure the lid to the cage is securely fastened, so the gerbils cannot escape.

Any holiday lasting more than three to four days requires the provision of a temporary carer to look after the gerbils during the owner's absence.

This is not a cumbersome burden by any means, but the temporary carer must be reliable. It will be their job to ensure that the gerbils are fed every day, that they have plenty of fresh water, that they remain safe in their cages, and that they cannot escape.

It goes without saying that the person you entrust with the care of your house and gerbils should be totally trustworthy and reliable.

Make sure the carer has the telephone number of your vet and a number on which you can be

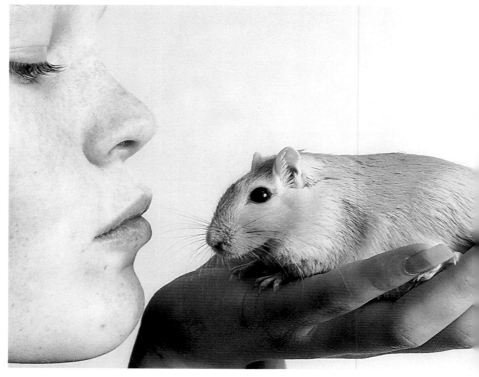

The caretaker must be someone who understands a gerbil's needs.

contacted in case of emergency. The ideal person is a good friend who can be safely entrusted with the house key.

Alternatively, some pet stores offer a small animal boarding service, where the gerbils are kept within the stores premises.

Remember to clean the gerbils' cage thoroughly before you go on holiday. This ensures the absence of bacteria in the cage, so that the gerbils should remain healthy while you are away. Don't forget to clean the cage thoroughly as soon as you return home.

To make things simple, you should place all the gerbil cages on the floor in one room. This ensures that no gerbil is missed out or 'forgotten'. Then, gather all the supplies and keep them near to the cages. The caretaker's job should be made as quick and simple as possible. Hopefully, if the job is easy, they will be willing to help you the next time.

You will need to explain to the caretaker exactly what you require. Give details about how much food should be given, where in the cage it should be placed, how to fill the water bottle and when to replace it, and how to check on the general hygiene of the cage.

Lastly, but by no means least, make sure the caretaker knows what to do in an emergency, e.g. when to call the vet, or how to catch an escaped gerbil.

Detailed, clear instructions will ensure that your gerbil is happy and healthy when you return home.

5 Gerbil Behaviour

Gerbils are known in the scientific community for their unique and interesting behaviour, which is constantly studied. Although every gerbil is unique, with a distinct personality of its own, there are certain gestures common to all gerbils. These gestures are strong indications of how the gerbil feels. If you take the time to familiarise yourself with the meanings of these gestures, you will be rewarded with a better understanding of, and a closer relationship with, your rodent friends.

GREETINGS

Gerbils greet each other by touching noses. In cages connected with plastic tunnels it is common to observe gerbils touching noses in the tunnels and when they first enter a room with another gerbil already in it. A secure and happy gerbil which trusts its owner may even rub noses with its owner. Before attempting this with your own gerbil, however, it is best to be sure, beyond doubt, that you have gained your gerbil's trust – otherwise you may end up getting your nose bitten!

Gerbils can develop strong pair-bonds.

TEETH CHATTERING

If a gerbil's teeth chatter together, it is normally a sign of anger. The gerbil should be returned to its cage and left alone for as much time as it takes for it to calm down. You will hear a gerbil's teeth chatter if you separate two fighting gerbils, or if two gerbils from different cages come into contact with each other.

If you hold a gerbil whose teeth are chattering, you will be able to feel the movement very clearly. You will probably also get bitten! Teeth chattering should not be confused with the sounds and movements made by a gerbil which is eating, although this can sound similar.

GNAWING

Gnawing is one of the most frequently exhibited behaviours of the gerbil. Your gerbil should always have something to gnaw on because gnawing is necessary to keep the teeth of a gerbil from growing too long and causing harm. However, gnawing can also indicate other feelings which your gerbil may be experiencing.

One reason gerbils gnaw is to create a nest in which to survive the cold winters by keeping warm. You will be able to tell if this is the reason your gerbil is gnawing because they will chew shavings and nesting material into tiny pieces and start creating a heap in the corner of the cage. The second reason gerbils chew is boredom. It is common to observe single gerbils doing this. Gnawing may also be a sign that the gerbil does not have enough space in its cage and is feeling very confined.

Gerbils will completely destroy anything made of plastic in the cage, by chewing it up into small pieces. Empty cotton reels make good gnawing blocks, but generally plastic is not a suitable material for anything which should not be gnawed (e.g. food bowl) – the temptation is too much for most gerbils.

WINKING

Winking (or to be more precise, blinking) can be a sign of affection from a gerbil. Gerbils are known to wink after they are given a treat from their owner. In some situations, a gerbil which winks may be displaying its submission to another gerbil or to you. If you blink at your gerbils when they are watching you, they should blink back. This is an excellent way to communicate with your gerbil, and when they wink back you may want to reward them with a treat.

FIGHTING

Fighting is a behavioural trait of the gerbil which has been well documented. Fighting is, unsurprisingly, a sign of aggression, usually related to a gerbil's territorial nature. This is especially true if an unfamiliar gerbil is put into the cage of another. For this reason, it is very important to introduce gerbils to each other slowly, carefully, and safely (see Chapter Three). When gerbils fight, they should be separated immediately if it looks at all likely that one may become injured.

LICKING

When gerbils need water, they may try to lick your hand or the walls of their cage. In the case of hand licking, it is thought that the gerbil is trying to absorb the moisture from their owner's hand, whereas cage licking is believed to be due to the gerbil's attempt to absorb the condensation on the sides of the cage.

If your gerbils start licking, check that the water bottle is functioning correctly. Gerbils may lick for no apparent reason, but, in most cases, lack of water is the cause.

EATING IN THE CORNER

Most of the time when food is put in the cage, a gerbil will take it, run to a corner of the cage, and then consume the food there. This is probably due to the gerbil trying to protect its food from other gerbils – a supposition borne out

The territorial gerbil will try to establish his dominance.

Gerbils are secretive about their food, and prefer to eat in the corner of the cage.

by the fact that when gerbils share food it is usually with their pair-bond or another gerbil with which they are on intimate terms.

ESCAPES AND CAPTURES

If you own a gerbil, the one event which you can be guaranteed to experience is that, at some point in time, your gerbil will escape. It appears to be inherent in gerbils to try to escape. Gerbils are masters of escapology, managing to find gaps in the most tightly closed cage lids. Fortunately, patterns of gerbil behaviour make it possible to effect a successful capture.

ESCAPE ROUTES

Any gerbil kept in a plastic cage has an open invitation to escape. Unless sufficient gnawing material is provided, the gerbil will chew on the plastic cage, eventually creating a hole through which it can escape. Any pet owner keeping a gerbil in a plastic cage should regularly check the cage for signs of chewing and developing holes.

One of the most common escape routes used by gerbils is through the cage lid. If it is not securely fastened, gerbils have even been known to force off the lid to the cage. It is also fairly common for gerbils to escape from the temporary home used when their cages are cleaned. For this reason, it is important to

As an escape artist, the gerbil is second to none!

ensure that the temporary container has a securely fitting lid.

LOCATION
If your gerbil manages to escape, attempts to recapture it must be made immediately, before it either injures itself or causes untold damage to your furnishings. Gerbils will not normally leave the room they are in immediately, but some can even climb stairs. If the gerbil has not been loose for long, it is most likely to be still in the room with the cage. It is therefore important to close all doors and windows before doing anything else. This will make them easier to locate and catch.

Gerbils are known to prefer dark places. This is probably due to their tunnelling instincts. Gerbil tunnels are dark and small, giving the gerbil a sense of security. Many gerbils return to the same place every time they escape.

If your gerbil has a favourite spot, you may be able to locate it straight away. If so, you can corner the gerbil and scoop it up in your hands. However, this may frighten the gerbil, who may either subsequently bite you, or jump, fall, and injure itself. The speed with which a gerbil can move may also render this approach useless. If you can catch a gerbil using this method then do so, but in most cases all that happens is that the gerbil escapes underneath an item of furniture, making capture harder than ever.

TRAPPING YOUR GERBIL
There will be times when, despite all your searching, you are simply unable to locate the whereabouts of your escaped gerbil. Gerbils can stay in the same small area (e.g.

underneath furniture) for a very long time, especially when they know you are trying to catch them. This means you may need to set a trap to catch your gerbil. There are many products available to catch pest rodents and pet rodents. However, not all of them are suitable for trying to catch a gerbil.

Be very careful when buying a trap. A mousetrap with a loaded spring is obviously intended to kill the mouse, but there are numerous other products available which are not so evident in their intention to kill or maim. It is best to use known humane traps that confine the gerbil to an inescapable place safely. Many of the traps intended for mice are too small for gerbils to get caught in, but some can work.

You may need to resort to setting a trap to catch your gerbil.

If you are unable to find anything suitable, it is possible to catch gerbils in home-made traps using simple materials. Gerbils have a keen sense of smell and this trait can be exploited to catch an escapee. A wastebasket with food in the bottom, set up with steps or a plank on the outside only (so that a gerbil can climb into it but cannot get out) makes a wonderful gerbil trap.

The escapee will often look for somewhere dark to hide.

6 Breeding

At some point in time, many gerbil owners decide to breed from their gerbils. From helping the gerbils to build a nest, preparing for the new litter, discovering the gerbils have been born, watching the babies grow up, and witnessing the transition the gerbils will make from naked, sightless new-borns to adult gerbils, there is much to see and delight in.

MAKING THE DECISION

Although breeding gerbils can bring money for some rarer colours, breeding gerbils is not generally a profitable pastime.

It is most likely that money spent on the additional cages needed to house the youngsters, and on the extra food, will far exceed the amount of money made by selling the babies.

Before being tempted to enter into breeding, you should bear in mind that the number and quality of the gerbil pups will decrease with every litter that each single gerbil female will produce.

To breed good gerbils consistently, several females will be required. With each female gerbil able to produce up to fifty baby gerbils in her lifetime, there are an awful lot of gerbils to provide homes for, should you decide to become a gerbil breeder.

REHOMING

Breeding gerbils should only be attempted if you have already guaranteed good homes for the new-borns. You may have lots of friends that want gerbils, or you may want more gerbils yourself, in which case no problems should arise.

However, do not rely on pet shops to buy your extra gerbils. Pet shops usually have a ready supply, and you are unlikely to receive any money for your youngsters, particularly when

You will need to plan ahead and find homes for all the gerbil babies.

gerbils with a known history and good longevity can be bought elsewhere from a breeder.

A BREEDER'S RESPONSIBILITY

A gerbil breeder must take responsibility for all the young produced. With a shortage of good homes available, many gerbils end up being rescued by animal charities, and far too many have to be put to sleep. You must be certain that your baby gerbils will receive proper care and attention in their new homes.

Above all, remember that the baby gerbils produced as a result of breeding your gerbils are your – the breeder's – responsibility. If you can meet the burdens placed by this responsibility, then breeding gerbils, whether as a full-time occupation or as a one-off event, will bring the caring owner much joy.

REPRODUCTIVE LIFE

Most female gerbils reach their sexual maturity at about three months old, although this can vary considerably from gerbil to gerbil. Some females will not produce their first litter until they are a year old, whereas others will become sexually active from as young as ten weeks. Once a female gerbil has become sexually active, she will normally remain so for about eighteen months. After this time, many females use up all their eggs (which promote sexual activity), and settle into a comfortable old age.

The number of litters a female gerbil may have can range from one to ten, with anything between three and nine pups in each litter. Although the size of each litter is particular to each individual gerbil, generally the litter size will decrease with every litter the female bears. This is because the female's fertility diminishes as she produces more pups.

Male gerbils become sexually active at three months, at around the same time as females. Unlike the female, the male can remain sexually active all of his adult life.

AGE AND CONDITION

Although some gerbils can reproduce at ten weeks of age, and most by three months, it is a good idea to make sure your gerbils are a little older than this. This is because the more time young gerbils are given to develop before they are bred from, the better parents they tend to make.

However, if you intend to breed, the mating pair should be put together and pair-bonded at about six to eight weeks of age.

There could be as few as three gerbil pups in a litter, or as many as ten.

Breeding stock must be chosen with the utmost care.

Although this seems rather young, attempts to pair older gerbils usually result in fighting. When the male and female are placed in the same cage at six weeks, it is unlikely that they will mate, as they are both too young, but a firm pair-bond is established, allowing for a more natural and less aggressive mating.

If you want to establish a strong male-female pair-bond between your proposed mating pair, but also want to delay the age at which the first litter is produced, this can be achieved by a wire-mesh cage-divider. This splits the cage vertically so that the gerbils can see and touch each other but are prevented from mating (see Adult Introductions, page 31).

However careful your preparations, and however keen you are to breed from your gerbils, you must be prepared to apply the brakes to the idea if there is any doubt about the gerbils' health, fitness and genetic quality.

Any gerbil used to breed must be of the highest standard, to be certain that the subsequent litter is healthy and of good quality, and to ensure that genetic conditions are not handed down to a new generation.

MATING

Mating occurs when the female is in heat, and receptive to the male's advances. This happens every four to six days, with the female gerbil remaining in heat for around 12 hours each time.

Mating usually occurs in the evening or the night, and will happen much more smoothly if the gerbils are kept in quiet, calm conditions – interference may result in both gerbils losing interest, or even turning on each other with aggression.

Mating is normally preceded by the male chasing the female around the cage for a few minutes. Eventually, the female will freeze, and will allow herself to be mounted by the male.

Intercourse lasts only for a few seconds, and is repeated many times over several minutes. Mating is usually accompanied by the male thumping his hind legs on the ground – a sign that he is excited.

After mating, you should begin to prepare for the new-born pups immediately.

It is difficult to determine pregnancy until a few days before the birth.

THE PREGNANT GERBIL

After mating, it can be difficult to determine whether the female is pregnant. Physical signs of pregnancy are not usually apparent until a few days before the birth, when the female's stomach enlarges in preparation for the birth. However, given the regularity with which mating will have occurred when the female was in heat, it is fairly safe to assume that the female gerbil is definitely pregnant once you have seen her mate with the male.

The average gerbil pregnancy lasts between 21 and 25 days, although this can vary considerably between gerbils. In some cases, such as where the female is still nursing her previous litter, pregnancy can be extended to over five weeks. Since pregnancy is difficult to determine, the best way of ensuring you are prepared for your gerbil's new litter is to mark down the mating days on a calendar. Then you will know to expect a litter in approximately 23 days.

CARING FOR THE MOTHER

During pregnancy, the most important contribution the owner can make is to improve the mother's diet. She should be given more protein to help the babies develop and to help prepare her for nursing. Scrambled egg or cheese provides plenty of extra protein, and even a small amount of cooked meat can help supply the pregnant gerbil with extra nutrients.

Another important point to consider is to be especially careful with the pregnant female. Handling should be kept to a minimum, and she should be given plenty of time alone when she is not being held. If the female suffers an injury caused by rough handling or dropping, her babies may die.

During the latter part of the pregnancy, it is sometimes helpful to remove the exercise wheel from

During pregnancy, the female will want to start preparing her nest for the birth.

the cage. This prevents the mother from over-exercising and damaging her babies.

PREPARING THE CAGE

From the time you believe the female to be pregnant, you will need to prepare the cage so that the female has as comfortable and healthy a pregnancy as possible. This will help ensure that there are no complications during birth, that a healthy litter is born, and that the female remains in good health. This is best achieved by the addition of plenty of protein-rich foods, as mentioned above, and plenty of extra nesting materials.

You should also check to make sure the cage is big enough to hold the new gerbils, allowing for approximately another four to eight gerbils in the cage. If not, the pregnant mother and the male should be moved to a new cage before the pregnancy has become too advanced. If they are moved late, this can prove extremely unsettling for the female, who can become quite distressed.

Towards the end of the pregnancy, extra materials should be added to the cage from which the mating pair can make a nest. Simple items such as cardboard toilet paper rolls and tissues work well. As soon as they are put in the cage the gerbils will chew them and will begin to use them to construct their nest.

BIRTHING

Gerbils will generally give birth without any complications, and do not usually require help. If complications do arise, it is necessary to seek assistance from a vet. The female giving birth will most likely die without immediate intervention, and, without their mother, the babies may die also.

A gerbil will usually give birth during the night or in the early morning. Labour tends to last for a few hours only. The owner will most likely miss the birth of the new-borns because of the time it

The pups are usually born during the night.

occurs, but it can still be very exciting to see and hear new-born baby gerbils when you look in the cage.

Before she gives birth, the female gerbil may make a large nest in part of the cage, signifying that birth is imminent. She will lie on her side licking herself, right up until the first baby is born. After the first pup emerges, the mother may move to another section of the cage and continue licking herself as the next pup is born. This process will continue until all the babies are delivered. Finally, the mother will gather all the babies and bring them into the nest.

The average number of gerbils in a litter is five or six, but gerbils frequently produce litters of between three and nine. The new-born pups will emit a constant high-pitched squeak, and if, after long periods of silence in the pregnant mother's cage, you hear this sound, it signifies that the birth has just taken place.

AFTER THE BIRTH

Directly after birth, the female comes into heat again. If the male is in the same cage, he and the female will mate immediately after the pups have been born and

At two weeks old, the pups have grown hair, but have still not opened their eyes.

secured in the nest. Although the female will not give birth to her next litter until the present one has been fully weaned (sometimes delaying birth by 43 days), she can become pregnant almost immediately after giving birth.

If you do not want the female to reproduce further, the main option is to separate the male and female, so that they are unable to mate. However, this is not always the best option. Male gerbils make excellent fathers, sharing the burden of responsibility with the mother. The father helps by retrieving any pups left at various points throughout the cage during labour. He also grooms them and helps to keep them warm while the mother is away looking for food and water for herself.

Do not remove the male if you wish to maintain the pair-bond between him and the mother. If your intention is to separate him from the female so that she does not become immediately pregnant again, and then to reintroduce him once her first in-heat phase has passed, you should remember that reintroductions may prove very difficult. The mother may become very aggressive towards the father, even if he has only been absent for three or four days. The female will be especially protective of her pups if she is rearing them alone, and any intrusion into her nest will be unwelcome and dealt with aggressively.

If you neither wish to remove the male gerbil, nor to have a second litter, neutering may be an option. However, it is not a common procedure among small animals, and finding a vet able or willing to perform the procedure may prove difficult.

CARING FOR THE PUPS

Baby gerbils are completely helpless when they are first born. Although they are born with whiskers, the pups are devoid of any other ability which would allow them to survive. They are born deaf, blind, toothless and hairless, and are completely reliant on their parents for their survival.

Both mother and father play an active role in rearing the pups.

This includes feeding and the provision of a constant source of body heat to prevent the pups dying from cold. The new-born pups require such attention that it is necessary to remove any and all distractions from the cage, if you have not already done so.

When the parent gerbils are happy and secure, they will make excellent parents, with the father playing an active role in the pups care.

As previously mentioned, if the mother is away from the nest for any reason, the father will stay with the pups to keep them warm and may also groom them.

Gerbil pups grow very rapidly. This four-week-old pup is well on the way to independence.

THE ROLE OF MUM

Despite the father's active involvement, a baby gerbil would soon die without the presence of the mother. This is due to the pup's dependence on its mother's milk. Up until a pup is weaned, it is fully dependent on the mother's milk, so loss of interest by the mother, or her death, would quickly result in the death of the litter.

It can be very hard to resist the temptation of constantly looking at and handling the gerbil pups, but it should be avoided at all costs. Handling the baby gerbils will rob them of their natural scent and replace it with a human scent. If this happens, the mother may refuse to care for the pups, and either abandon them or kill them.

Likewise, frequent interruption and lack of privacy may cause the mother significant stress, which, at its most extreme, may result in her eating her pups. Although this is not common, care should be taken to avoid the possibility from ever occurring.

If you notice that the litter seems to be decreasing in number, or if you actually witness the mother eating her young, despite the fact that she has been left alone and not placed under stress as far as you are aware, think of diet. Consuming her own young is sometimes a symptom of malnutrition, particularly protein deficiency, in the post-natal gerbil. This can be compensated for by introducing mealworms into the nursing gerbil's diet.

The gerbil pups grow very rapidly. After about five days, the pups will begin to grow hair. Pups which are patched or pied may have clear 'birth-spots', which indicate where the fur is going to be white.

Within two weeks the gerbils will have a full coat of fur, and you should be able to determine their sex. By the time they are nine weeks old the gerbils have reached adolescence. By 12 weeks they are almost fully adult and most are capable of reproducing.

WEANING

The gerbil pups should be fully weaned by the time they are four to six weeks of age. The mother gerbil will wean them from her milk, and the responsibilities of the owner lie only in ensuring that enough high-quality food is available to the mother and the pups.

Within two weeks of being born, the pups will gradually

decrease the amount of breast milk in their diet in favour of more solids. The less milk they consume at this young age, the higher the risk of them missing essential nutrients.

In young gerbils, where the immune system is not fully developed, this can have far-reaching effects. If the gerbils do not receive all the nutrients they require, they are susceptible to respiratory infections as youngsters, and more vulnerable than most to various ailments as adults.

During the weaning stage of a young gerbil's life, it may be a good idea to give the young gerbils vitamins and certain treats that are

The mother gerbil will wean her pups between the ages of four and six weeks.

By six weeks, the pups are fully grown and can go to their new homes.

designed for gerbils, and can be purchased at most pet stores.

The gerbils should be given treats to make up for some of the nutrients they have become deprived of while not getting their mother's milk.

The pups should be fully independent by four to six weeks of age, and at this point they can be given away, or put in a cage without their parents.

Because not all gerbils become fully independent at the same time, you should watch closely to make sure the gerbils are not nursing any longer before you separate them from their mother. If you notice that the gerbils are still nursing, it is a definite sign that they cannot yet be separated from their mum, and you should wait until nursing has finished before doing so.

7 *Colours And Genes*

Colour mutation is rare among gerbils. However, since gerbils have been kept in captivity, many new colours have emerged. World-wide selective breeding has produced many new colours which are unknown in the wild. The prospective owner can now choose from dozens of varieties.

THE ROLE OF GENES

Colour variations occur as the result of a mutation of the gene governing colour. The mutation will either alter the existing gene, which will then produce a variation on an existing colour, or the gene will mutate to such an extent that, in effect, it becomes a new gene, producing a new and unique colour.

If a gerbil with a mutated colour gene is bred with a gerbil of a different colour, more new colours can be produced. The mutated gene interacts with the other colour gene to create a new gene. Breeding gerbils for colour can be a very interesting and exciting hobby. It can be extremely rewarding to see the development of a rare colour, when the new-

Gerbils come in many colours. Pictured (left to right): silver, golden and grey.

born gerbil pups start to grow fur.

Rare colours can be achieved through careful planning. Knowing the genes of each individual gerbil in the breeding stock allows the breeder to predict which colours will occur when two of those gerbils are mated to produce a litter. This can be achieved through the use of a 'punnet' square. These allow the colour genes to be plotted against each other so that colour outcome can be determined.

COLOUR GENES

To date, there are seven genes (loci) known to affect colour. The seven located loci are: A, C, E, G, P, Sp, and D, and all may be dominant or recessive. If dominant, the gene is represented by a capital letter, and if recessive, it is represented by a lower-case letter. Each gene is responsible for influencing a particular aspect of a gerbil's colour and appearance.

Each parent gerbil contributes a copy of one colour-governing gene to each pup within the litter. Depending on which gene this is, whether or not it is dominant or recessive, and how it mixes with the counterpart gene from the other parent, different colours may result.

AGOUTI PATTERNS

Agouti patterns affect the individual hairs of the gerbil. Agouti gerbils have hairs which change colour in bands from root to tip. This usually takes the following form: dark at the root base; a sandy-coloured band around the centre of the hair; and a dark tip. Agouti-patterned gerbils frequently have a white underbelly.

The 'A' locus determines whether or not the gerbil will possess the agouti pattern. If 'A' is a dominant gene in either parent, only one parent needs to possess and pass on this gene in order for the offspring to be born with agouti patterns. If the gerbil receives a recessive 'a' from both gerbils, each hair on the gerbil will be completely black from root to tip.

Agouti patterns are quite common. Pictured: Golden Agouti.

DARK SPOTS

A gerbil's coat is generally one colour (although the underside can differ). However, within that general colour, there can be variations – usually lighter or darker versions of the main colour. The Burmese Gerbil, for example, has darker-coloured fur on its nose, hands and feet. Gerbils with dark spots such as these are sometimes referred to as 'colourpoints'.

The 'C' locus plays a large role in determining whether a gerbil will have dark spots. If 'c' is present in a recessive form in one parent, which is then mated with another gerbil possessing the same recessive gene, the resulting litter will have dark spots.

However, the recessive form of 'c' is quite rare. It is usually present in dominant form, which does not produce darker areas of fur.

LIGHT SPOTS

The 'E' locus, like the 'C' locus, produces colour spots. In dominant form, 'E' produces dark spots at the root-base of the hair. However, in its recessive form, it can produce many different, lighter shades.

The recessive 'e' produces gerbils which are fox-coloured. The gerbil pup will be born with the pigmentation to produce reddish-orange fur. As the gerbil ages, this colour will fade, gradually becoming increasingly pale. Older fox gerbils can sometimes appear white.

GOLDEN

One of the most common coloured gerbils is the golden agouti. As its name suggests, the golden agouti takes its name from the golden/sandy-coloured middle section of the agouti-patterned hair. The 'G' locus in its dominant form is responsible for this.

GREY

In its recessive form, 'g' produces a grey colour. In grey agouti gerbils, the yellow band is replaced

A gerbil with grey agouti fur.

with grey-coloured hair, which produces a completely different effect.

BLACK OR WHITE
Dark-coloured gerbils with dark eyes have the dominant form of the 'P' locus. This gene gives the gerbil dark eyes and hair which is black at base and tip. As a general rule, gerbils with dark eyes nearly always have dark fur.

The recessive form of 'p' produces pale-coloured gerbils. Older fox gerbils are sometimes mistakenly referred to as having the recessive 'p' locus. True 'p' gerbils have very light or white fur, with pale eyes.

White gerbils with pink eyes are sometimes thought to be albinos, but this is not the case. Albinos, or Ruby-Eyed White as they are known otherwise, have a different gene combination altogether.

WHITE SPOTS
White spots appear in the gerbil's coat in much the same manner as dark spots. The difference is that the 'Sp' locus is responsible for producing white spots.

These patches of white fur can occur in many places, and the exact location varies greatly.

The distinctive-looking black gerbil.

The Ruby-Eyed White (Albino) gerbil should not be confused with the Pink-Eyed White.

Patches are known to occur on the front and back of the neck, back, hands and feet, as well as on the base of the tail.

Although these patches occur in many different places, some patterns are evident with much more frequency, such as the shape of an arrow on the back of the gerbil's neck.

The blue gerbil is very rare.

'BLUE' OR 'DILUTE'

'Dilute' gerbils are the only true 'blue' gerbils, and are exceptionally rare. Only a few are known to exist in northern and western Europe. The 'Dilute' gerbil has only been recognised since 1997, when the 'Dilute' or 'D' gene was discovered. The 'D' gene controls the depth of colour of the gerbil's coat, making the colour either more vibrant or pale, depending on whether or not the gene is dominant or recessive.

The recessive 'd' gene dilutes the strength of all the colours seen in the gerbil's coat. When the 'd' gene was first discovered, selective breeding produced the first true blue gerbil. The slate gerbil may often appear to be blue, but it is not a true blue gerbil like the one created by the Dilute gene.

The Burmese is one of the many varieties produced in breeding programmes.

COLOUR GENES

Gerbils have been bred for many years in dozens of different colours and varieties. Most of these colour variations are represented in the chart below. Included within the chart are the genes responsible for producing each colour, together with details as to whether or not the genes are dominant or recessive.

COLOUR	GENE COMBINATION
Agouti	A*, P*, C*, G*, E*
Agouti Grey	A*, P*, C*, gg, E*
Apricot	A*, pp, C*, gg, ee
Argente Golden	A*, pp, CC, G*, E*
Argente Nutmeg	aa, pp, C*, G*, ee
Black	aa, P*, C*, G*, E*
Burmese	aa, P*, cbcb, G*, E*
Dark-Eyed Honey (DEH)	A*, P*, C*, G*, ee
Dark-Tailed White (DTW)	**, P*, chch, **, E*
Dove	aa, pp, Cch, G*, E*
Lilac	aa, pp, CC, G*, E*
Nutmeg	P*, C*, G*, ee
Pink-Eyed White (PEW)	**, pp, chch, **, E*
Polar Fox	A*, P*, C*, gg, ee
Ruby-Eyed White (REW)	aa, pp, C*, gg, E*
Schimmel	**, P*, CC, G*, efef
Siamese	aa, P*, cbch, G*, E*
Slate	aa, P*, C*, gg, E*
Yellow Fox	A*, pp, C*, G*, ee

NB: A star represents the fact that the missing locus can be either dominant or recessive without affecting the outcome of the gerbil's coloration. White spots are not covered in this table, since they have little effect in the overall appearance of the gerbil's coat. Also, the Dilute gene is not included because it is so rare.

8 *Health Care*

Even though gerbils are able to care for themselves to a large extent, it is not uncommon for them to develop certain complaints. Most of these will clear up by themselves, but if, after a few days, they are still present or are causing the gerbil distress, veterinary assistance should be sought.

VET VISITS

A gerbil owner should be fully prepared for any emergency before it occurs. One of the most useful preparations you can make is to have to hand a piece of paper with your vet's name, address, and telephone number. It is important to ensure that the vet has considerable experience in treating small animals.

TRAVELLING

When taking gerbils to the vet, the small plastic cages usually reserved for iguanas make excellent travelling boxes.

To prepare the travelling box, some of the current wood shavings from the gerbil's main cage should be placed in the bottom of the box. It helps to include some of the gerbil's droppings with the shavings. Not only will this reassure the gerbil,

but the vet is also able to observe the droppings – an important diagnostic factor.

The gerbil should always be kept warm while he is taken to the vet, and extra measures should be taken to ensure that he is under no extra stress for any reason. Gerbils dislike travelling by car, so it is important to make sure they are well strapped in and are jostled no more than is necessary. When travelling, the water bottle should be removed. This is because the motion of the vehicle may cause it to leak and worsen the gerbil's condition.

DIAGNOSIS

The vet may ask many questions about the health and daily routine of the gerbil. These are important for his diagnosis and treatment. It is therefore helpful if you are able for provide as much information as possible about: daily routine and feeding; any recent changes; and possible symptoms (e.g. a sudden cough), etc. You should also pass on information about other gerbils in the same cage, such as whether or not they are experiencing any symptoms.

Needless to say, the vast majority of illnesses your gerbil may suffer are likely to clear up by themselves with no veterinary assistance required. Some of the most common complaints particular to gerbils are listed below.

BROKEN LIMBS

Broken limbs are very common with gerbils. Sometimes they may occur as a result of a fall, trapping a leg, or fighting, but, equally, they seem to appear for no apparent reason. Although most breaks are uncomplicated and heal well, you should always consult a vet.

Most of the time, the vet will only check over the gerbil, and

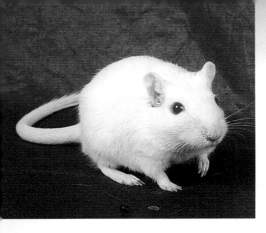

then allow the break to heal naturally. However, although the vet may not seem to do a great deal, you should always take a gerbil suffering with a broken limb along to be assessed.

Sometimes, infection can arise in the break, which requires a course of antibiotics to be prescribed by the vet.

If the break is very nasty, there may be nothing which can help. Gerbils are very small creatures, and, as such, surgery is not always possible. It is difficult to perform successfully, and gerbils frequently die from the effects of the anaesthesia. Fortunately, most breaks are not this serious – requiring time alone to heal.

ASSISTING RECOVERY

There are a few additional things which you can do to speed up the healing process. Remove the exercise wheel from the gerbil's cage, so that it is forced to take things easy for a while.

If the gerbil is unable to move very far, ensure that it has easy access to food and water (which may mean adjusting the height of the water bottle), as a well-nourished gerbil will heal far quicker than a gerbil which is weak through lack of food and water.

Most breaks heal without complication, and the gerbils will normally have made a full recovery within two weeks. Occasionally, the bone may not heal straight, but this does not seem to present too much of a problem to most gerbils.

A break can be a sign of a lack of minerals such as calcium in the diet, which, as with humans, is important to maintain strong and healthy bones. If your gerbil breaks a leg, carefully examine its diet. If you think your gerbil needs more calcium, you can supplement its diet with dog food or special gerbil treats made from yoghurt (available in most pet shops).

COLDS

Gerbils can catch colds from their human owners, so it is important to stay away from the gerbils if you have any sneezes or a cough, etc. You should also be careful to avoid contact with their food.

Food should be poured straight from the bag into the bowl or cage floor, so that germs are not passed on to the gerbils through contact with the bacteria on your hands.

Symptoms of a cold in gerbils include a runny nose, and a high-pitched sneeze. If your gerbil has a cold, it should be kept in a warm room, allowing it plenty of time to recover. If its condition does not improve within a few days, take it to your vet.

DIARRHOEA

Diarrhoea is a very common complaint in gerbils, because it can occur due to a simple imbalance of diet. The most common cause is too many green leafy vegetables, and not enough dry food. To cure diarrhoea, the gerbils should be fed dry food mix only for a while, with no vegetables. A gradual decrease in the amount of vegetables given will only prolong the period of suffering for the gerbil. The change in diet should stop the diarrhoea, but, if it continues, then the help of a vet should be sought.

INNER EAR PROBLEMS

Inner ear problems are a common occurrence in the older gerbil. The problem is caused by cholesteatoma, an untreatable cyst. The most recognisable feature of inner ear problems is the tilting of the gerbil's head. Other symptoms

include loss of balance and running around in circles.

If you think your gerbil is suffering from an inner ear problem, take it to your vet, as many cases are easily curable. The problem usually stems from an infection, which can be treated by a one-off antibiotic injection. Never leave the problem to clear up by itself. Left untreated, this condition can lead to death.

MITES

Mites are a constant enemy as far as gerbils are concerned. Gerbils can contract mites from many things, and, once contracted, the mites irritate the gerbils a great deal.

The most common manner in which gerbils contract mites is through their food. Many forms of food contain mites anyway, but even uncontaminated food can eventually attract mites. The mites live in the food until it is put in the cage, at which point they attack the gerbils.

The best way to try to eradicate mites from the gerbils' food supply is to freeze all the food until shortly before it is due to be given to the gerbils.

Gerbils can also contract mites from anything put in their cage which has been outdoors. For this reason, it is important to wash everything thoroughly before it is put in the cage.

Sometimes, despite the best efforts of the owner, a gerbil will still develop a problem with mites. If this happens, the signs are usually very clear. The gerbil will scratch a lot, as if it has fleas, and in many cases the mites themselves will be clearly obvious in the cage.

Mites are tiny little red or black bugs, which stand out because there are usually many of them, rather than just one or two which

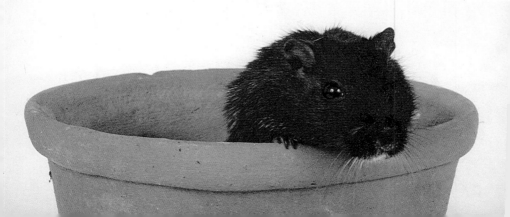

may be difficult to see. In most cages where there is a mite infestation, hundreds of mites will be seen scurrying around the cage.

Fortunately, mites are relatively easy to eradicate. Most pet shops sell sprays which can be used to kill the mites. Firstly, the gerbils should be sprayed and then placed in a thoroughly clean and sterile travelling box to dry off.

While the gerbils are drying, the cage should be washed with a disinfectant solution and sprayed as well. This should solve the problem.

TEETH

A gerbil's teeth never stop growing. For this reason, it is very important to provide your gerbils with plenty of suitable gnawing materials (wooden blocks; cotton reels, preferably made of wood; and even special gnawing 'treats', which are flavoured) so that the teeth can be worn down.

If there is plenty to chew on, most gerbils will not have a problem with their teeth when they are young.

However, older gerbils tend to gnaw less, and frequently end up with overlong or broken teeth, and these need to be treated. Left untreated, the gerbil may develop mouth abscesses which are very painful, and the animal may even starve to death if the teeth prevent it from eating.

Broken teeth need to be helped to grow back to normal length and shape. A vet will need to monitor this. Overgrown teeth can be treated, with much more immediate results, by a vet who will clip them to a more appropriate length.

If the gerbil's teeth need to be clipped regularly, get your vet to demonstrate how to clip a gerbil's teeth before you attempt it yourself.

RESPIRATORY INFECTIONS

When young gerbils are weaned, it is important that their first solids contain the same amount of nutrients found in their mother's milk. If those nutrients are not present, the gerbils can grow up to become prone to infection.

In younger gerbils, this usually manifests as a respiratory infection, the symptoms of which include laboured breathing and a clicking sound whenever the gerbil draws in breath. There are many over-the-counter remedies to cure this, but, if the problem persists, you should contact a vet.

SCENT GLAND TUMOURS

Scent gland tumours are generally more likely to occur in older male gerbils. This is due to the fact that male gerbils are more territorial, and use their scent gland more frequently than females to mark their territory. However, there are reports of occurrences in females.

The tumours begin as a small pinkish-coloured lump, appearing on the yellow scent gland on the underside of the gerbil. The tumour will grow in size until it starts to irritate the gerbil. The gerbil usually responds by biting off the tumour, which will soon grow back. When you first notice a tumour, you should take your gerbil to the vet.

If the tumour grows to be too large and irritates the gerbil a great deal, then surgery can be considered. Not all gerbils will survive surgery, which is a very expensive option, but it may be a decision you have to make. Your vet will normally explain all the options available, before letting you make the decision.

Tumours may occur on parts of the body other than the scent gland, but this is rare. Unfortunately, internal tumours cannot be operated upon, and, in cases when it is apparent that the gerbil is suffering, it is better to have it put painlessly to sleep by a vet.

SORE NOSES

A sore nose seems to be a species characteristic of the gerbil. A gerbil may develop a sore nose because of many things, but it is most commonly caused by allergies.

The gerbil may develop a skin irritation on its nose from the oils in pine or cedar bedding. To prevent this, a different type of bedding should be used, such as aspen. Soreness caused by allergies can also occur in the gerbil's eyes.

Sometimes, a gerbil may develop loss of fur around its nose, as well as soreness. This is usually the result of chewing on the metal bars of the cage, which rub away the fur when the gerbil pokes its nose between the bars.

Keeping your gerbils in an aquarium rather than a metal-wire cage will normally cure this. Removing all irritants and allowing the nose time to heal is

all that is necessary most of the time.

However, if, despite your best efforts, your gerbil still has a sore nose, consult your vet – it may be the case that your gerbil has an unknown allergy.

STROKES

Strokes occur mostly in older gerbils, much as they do in humans. Symptoms include partial paralysis, weakness of one or more limbs, or weakness down one side. As an owner, the first symptom you may notice is that your gerbil is walking around the cage leaning heavily to one side.

There is no cure for a gerbil suffering from a stroke. The best treatment is to help the gerbil as much as possible with its daily routine, including help with feeding. The gerbil should remain as comfortable as possible to help speed the recovery.

Unfortunately, a second stroke, shortly after the first, is not an uncommon occurrence, and it usually causes death. However, it is also possible for a gerbil to lead a normal healthy life after a stroke, provided that it is well cared for.

TAIL LOSS

Gerbils have very fragile tails that

can easily be lost in an injury. Normally, only part of the tail is lost. If your gerbil loses part of its tail, you will probably notice that a certain length of healthy tail is left, with a short length of bone exposed from the part which has been lost. Once the exposed bone has dried, the gerbil will remove it, and the wound normally heals up very well. Although this looks very unpleasant, it is not serious.

A gerbil will not suffer from only having a partial tail, and, in most cases, balance does not seem to be affected too much.

However, if your gerbil loses the whole of its tail, you should take it straight to the vet. Loss of the entire tail can cause problems with balance and places the gerbil at a much higher risk of serious infection. If the whole tail is missing there is frequently a nasty wound at the base, which the vet should close and disinfect to avoid any further harm to the gerbil.

WET TAIL

Although wet tail is most common in hamsters, it is known to occur in gerbils also. Wet tail is very often confused with diarrhoea, but is a much more serious illness.

It is caused by an imbalance of bacteria in the stomach of the gerbil, which causes a much more extreme form of diarrhoea, along with a strong, unpleasant odour.

Another symptom that distinguishes wet tail from diarrhoea is a sticky wet look around the anus of the gerbil. Without treatment, it can spread to the base of the tail. If any of the symptoms of wet tail are shown, then it is best to seek advice from a vet, because wet tail can very easily be fatal. The vet will most likely prescribe a wide variety of antibiotics, hoping to cure wet tail.

WOUNDS

Wounds usually occur as a result of fighting between gerbils. They

are usually not too serious and in most cases will heal themselves.

To avoid infection, all wounds should be treated with an antibiotic, or hydrogen peroxide, which will kill any bacteria. Administering this can be quite tricky.

The anti-bacterial agents will sting when applied to the gerbil, and it is quite likely that you will get bitten. One way to avoid this is to wear soft gloves (nothing too heavy-duty or you will not be able to feel how tight you are holding the gerbil – be sure not to squeeze).

Put some antibiotic on a cotton bud and gently dab the wound with it.

In most cases, this will be all the treatment required, but for anything more serious you may wish to contact your vet.